ELLE DECOR: THE GRAND BOOK OF FRENCH STYLE

First North American Edition

ISBN 0-8212-2764-5

Library of Congress Control Number 2001088800

Bulfinch Press is an imprint and trademark of Little, Brown and Company (Inc.)

Translation: Translate-A-Book, Oxford, England

Translated text © Cassell & Co, 2001

PRINTED IN FRANCE BY CLERC

ELLE DECOR: THE GRAND BOOK OF FRENCH STYLE

FRANÇOIS BAUDOT

AND

JEAN DEMACHY

A Bulfinch Press Book

Little, Brown and Company

Boston • New York • London

SEVEN TRENDS FOR TODAY (p. 8)

SIX PARISIAN FASHION DESIGNERS AT HOME (p. 180)

EIGHT PARISIAN INTERIOR DESIGNERS AT HOME (p. 220)

The Elements of a *style*

In the biblical legend, Asmodeus is an evil spirit who lifts the roofs off houses in order to create chaos inside. We, too, lift the roofs off houses, but our aim is quite the reverse. For more than 15 years, *Elle Décoration* magazine has been suggesting to its readers a thousand and one ideas on how to harmonize elements in what is the best part of their lives – the part they spend with their family, in the garden, traveling, or by the fireside. The only possible demon is that of curiosity in the face of the eternal questions: how do others live, and how can we ourselves live differently, meaning in a better way?

Every house has its own personality, as do the people who live in it. But the houses whose roofs we lift off here – and their inhabitants – are far from being immune to fashion, even if by "fashion", we mean "a way of life." As you leaf through these pages, *Elle Déco* (to give it its popular title) doesn't intend to add its own style to those of others. We aren't trying to write a grammar book on style. Our aim is to observe trends. And to take account of them with a new and original eye, that of our magazine. *Elle Déco*'s style is simply to observe with neither pretention nor neutrality.

We have divided this book into thematic chapters to aid readability. With very few exceptions, we have restricted our examples to France, because France, more than anywhere else, is a place where trends, cultures, and their differences converge in a stimulating way. For they are absorbed, integrated, digested, and reframed in accordance with France's own types and categories. The influence of Asia, Africa, Anglo-America, the exoticism of travel to faraway places, eclectic trends, the love of the past – all these currents and many others mingle in the sort of "Happy Families" card game that *Elle Décoration* essentially is. A certain idea of decoration is necessary: the first principle is to forget all others. Faithful to the philosophy of its flagship *Elle*, this book advocates that the useful should be beautiful and that the inspiring should be available at all prices. None of the pictures here imposes anything. However, each has some kind of message – an idea to come back to, an example to think about, according to one's own home and budget.

To this journey through the "interior life", we have added two complementary chapters. One suggested itself, because it describes the way in which some notable interior designers have arranged their own environments for living. These interior architects are by profession the great catalysts for any evolution or new trend, and that is nowhere else better expressed than in their own personal living spaces. As for couturiers, fashion designers and stylists, the privileged relationships our group has with them often means that we are most fortunate to be able to look inside their private domains. The ways in which these creators view garments often extends to their own environments for living. So the world of this book reaches from the decorative arts across to the art of fashion. Its many facets unify here to constitute a style. It is the sum of all the others: the style within this book.

J.D, F.B.

*1930s and 40s*style

The final decades of the 20th century saw the decorative arts of the interwar period become one of the liveliest fields of inspiration, discovery, and collectibility. In the early 1980s came the rediscovery of Jean-Michel Frank (1895–1941), whose work is now universally imitated. Such is the remarkable reevaluation of the decorative artists, the interior designers, and the craftsmen of the 1930s and 1940s that their work is now viewed alongside the finest products of design coming from areas like ethnic art or historic furniture. The criteria shared by all the elements in this mosaic of trends are the quality and discreet charm attributed to times that have passed.

The library in Yves Saint-Laurent's apartment, decorated by Jacques Grange. Between two windows an oil painting by Fernand Léger hangs above the Le Corbusier steel console bearing a hammered-silver box, a 1925 vase, and an African statuette.

The history of styles is a story of continual revival. Aside from reasons of economy and aesthetics, prompting many of our contemporaries to scour the Marché aux Puces – the largest and oldest fleamarket in Paris – and antique or junk shops to furnish their interiors, fashions come and go. All the while they regularly influence the market, the prices of objects and, eventually, the art of interior design. The second half of the 20th century has witnessed a frenetic rereading of the decorative arts of the first half. Art Nouveau and then Art Deco have thus been appreciated the second time around at least as much as they were during their creators' own periods. Certain exceptional pieces have reached prices even higher than the finest 18th-century objects.

And quite rightly so. Some of these modern pieces have as much quality, originality, and rarity value even, as the most prestigious works of the cabinet-makers, ornamentalists, or craftsmen of the Age of Enlightenment.

The eccentric few, be they artists, lawyers, couturiers, or the merely curious, who in the 1960s – to the bemusement of many – combed the newly emergent bric-à-brac merchants for perhaps a Gallé vase or a chair by Ruhlmann, now belong to the highest echelons of collectors. Retro style has influenced an entire era. Contributing to the trend were the appeal of off-the-rack clothes and 1960s decor: from neo-Tiffany to the cubism of the TV-sofa, via a whole cinema (Borsalino and Company).

Buoyed by success, the young dealers specializing in the 1930s have

Between the abstractness of 20th-century avant-garde and the starkness and purity of returning Neoclassicism, cabinet-makers, wrought-iron artists, interior designers, and painters of the interwar period managed to steer a middle course between modernist coolness and the unvarying elements of French tradition.

abandoned the Porte de Clignancourt, where the Marché aux Puces is located, or Les Halles for the inner sanctum of the pioneers of Art Nouveau and Art Deco: the area between the Rue de Seine and Rue Bonaparte.

Now that such modern antiques are outside the price range of incoming collectors, the children of the age of advertising are looking to an even more recent period: the 1950s. From the earliest juke boxes to American cast-off stock, you can get hold of whatever you want from the kitsch of the 1950s, and there is quality, too, that would do credit to any collection.

As for the the way pop culture has emerged in decoration, this has led to highly individual expression. Often aggressive in their bad taste, the exponents of that specific retro fashion might find themselves more at home

Jean-Michel Frank surrounded by friends in the shop in the Rue du Faubourg Saint-Honoré. From left to right: A. Giacometti, J.-M. Frank, E. Terry, Rodochanachi, C. Bérard, A. Chanaux, D. Giacometti.

in a sociological study than in a magazine of decoration.

However, they evidently don't interest today's enthusiasts, who in their keenness to renew acquaintance with the great tradition of past decorative artists have turned instead to the 1930s and 1940s. For, until the 1990s, our own period seemed to have forgotten that particular stage in the history of styles. As it needed a name, it was given that of the "40s". This ambiguous title itself explains the awkward, even downtrodden, reputation of that period of decoration. For many families in 1940, interior decoration was just about one of the last things on their minds.

The fact is that the so-called "40s" style actually went back to the mid-30s, and carried on into the late 50s. The "40s" art of decoration was less creative than earlier styles, and is therefore harder to define. Moreover, one hesitates sometimes to dub as

Large lounge in the mansion of Vicount and Vicountess Charles de Nouailles in Paris (Jean-Michel Frank).

"antique" (and price accordingly) products originating from Ramsay, Baguès, Spade, Devoluy, and so on – all businesses whose showcases, seemingly only yesterday, epitomized to youthful and rebellious eyes the worst bourgeois conventions.

Yet as time passes, over and over again we have seen previous judgments revised. The pendulum swings for every fashion. And the inescapable

reality is that after a period of rejection – a period which seems to get ever shorter – the fashion reappears and is widely acclaimed.

As modernism advances, so our appetite for times gone by seems to grow. The "40s" style is a concrete expression of the last great period of French artisanship, with its expertise, its cult of classicism, and its innate sense of the finely finished.

How sad it is that the company of great furniture-makers, those heirs to the cabinet-markers of the Ancien Régime, neither resisted nor came to terms with mass production, the system imposed by new trademarks such as Knoll, Mobilier International, Herman Miller, and others. It is indisputable that, against their plurality, the "40s" style was actually a last stand for individuality.

Opposite, left: A small lounge in the Guerlain house in the Champs-Elysées (1939); *Trompe-l'œil* by C. Bérard.

Opposite, right: The entrance to the Harriet Hubbard Ayer Institut de Beauté, Faubourg Saint-Honoré. Wrought-iron gates by Gilbert Poillerat; ceramic caryatid by Jouve, 1948.

Previous two pages
Twin fireplaces in Joseph Ettedgui's
lounge where an Eileen Gray lacquer
screen separates the two halves; 1920s
and 30s furniture; Perzel lamps; and
Lalique vases. In the foreground is an
Art Deco period bronze.

Above and right
This vestibule/dining room is lit by
two André Dubreuil crystal and steel
girandoles which stand on a large Art
Deco steel console from the gallery of
David Gill. The lacquered leather
furniture dates from the 1930s. The

vases on the console and table end are
Lalique glassware. In the foreground is
a magnificent "snake" standard-lamp
created by Brandt in bronze and streaked
glass. The chairs are in Ruhlman style.
The floor itself is simple: old flagstones
have been sanded and polished.

Above

In the French Foreign Ministry building is a bathroom designed by the Compagnie des Arts Français in 1938 for the visit of King George VI and Queen Elizabeth of Great Britain. A tripartite mirror reflects the wall motifs with their encrusted studs of shattered glass.

Right

The Roman bathtub with mosaics and silver handles is surrounded by a shattered-glass motif by Labouré. On either side are two white leather stools with silver framework designed by Adnet. The white swans are by Lalique.

Marble-topped console
with molded palm-form
plaster legs, a creation
of Serge Roche. The
sculpture and ceramic
candelabras are from the
Néo-Senso collection
(Sèvres manufactory).

Left

Monaco. in the Monte
Carlo Star block. The
drawing room assembled
by Karl Lagerfeld in the
spirit of the 1940s.
Day-bed and carpet
designed in 1938 by
André Arbus; sculptures
by Delamare and
Belmondo; a pair of Arbus
armchairs covered in olive
green leather.

Following two pages

Paris. in the home of
a collector with an
enthusiasm for the
1940s and 1950s.
In the downstairs part of
the large drawing room.
a pillar supports the
mezzanine. The large sofa
and armchairs by André
Arbus sit on an Arbusson
carpet. The cartoon is by
Jacques Despierre (1948).
In front of the windows is
a table with crossing legs
designed by Arbus and a
pair of mirror obelisks by
Poillerat. The furniture
as a whole is from the
Yves Gastou gallery. Paris.

Above
The large wrought-iron pedestal table is by Gilbert Poillerat.
On the marble top are two studies in terra-cotta by the sculptor
Raymond Dellamare. Behind can be glimpsed a piece in green
lacquer by Jacques Quinet. The 1940s furniture is from the
Yves Gastou gallery.

Right
In this 18th century private mansion, Yves Gastou has
included 1940s wrought-iron work. The gilded chandelier
is by Jean Royère: the pair of chandeliers by Zadkine (for Marc
Duplantier). The piece between the windows in 18th century
gilded wood bears a pair of Chinese gourd table lamps.

Left

Above the painted iron console in the entrance to the apartment of antiques specialist Alexandre Biaggi there is a rare witch's mirror in resin, designed by Line. Vautrin in the 1940s. The small chairs are in polished bronze. while the plaster vase. sea shells. mask. and decorative motifs were bought at the Marché aux Puces.

Above

In Alexandre Biaggi's home. zinc geometric shapes surround an anonymous picture-object in paper. iron wire. and wax.

Fine bathroom in 1940s
style with furniture
designed by Jean Royère.
Pedestal table by Du
Plantier. The bathtub is
set into the marble of the
floor. Furniture from the
Yves Gastou gallery.

Left
Against a mirror background, a charming pair of Venetian lanterns, designed
by Barovier and Toso, adorn a 1940s
half-moon console in the octagonal
dining room of a Parisian collector.

Above
A vase-light has been created from
minutely worked Venetian glass, and
it dominates the sculpted wrought-iron
pediment of a play cabinet which was
designed by Gilbert Poillerat.

Following two pages
In this dining room is a collection of
chairs by Jean Royère: on either side is
a Pierre Lardin console. On the window
sills are two antique terra-cotta busts,
between them a bronze head of Venus.

31

*Eccentric*style

They are free spirits. They don't give a thought to the rationalist rules of the international style that have held sway for almost a century. Today, eccentricity of decor consists essentially in strangeness, in thinking that the shortest distance between two points is not a straight line. This is real glasshouse culture, the busy whimsicality of a few designers with a sense of humor. Its very apartness makes the creativity of this style one of the most important elements in contemporary decorative arts.

In David Gill's home, a giant Garouste and Bonetti mirror with gold-leaf gilding is suspended like a pendulum from the ceiling. It reflects a "Novogorod" chest of drawers from the same designers, a unique piece in gilded wood with bronze feet and handles.

A plaster plinth with bust, Orielle Harwood (1994).

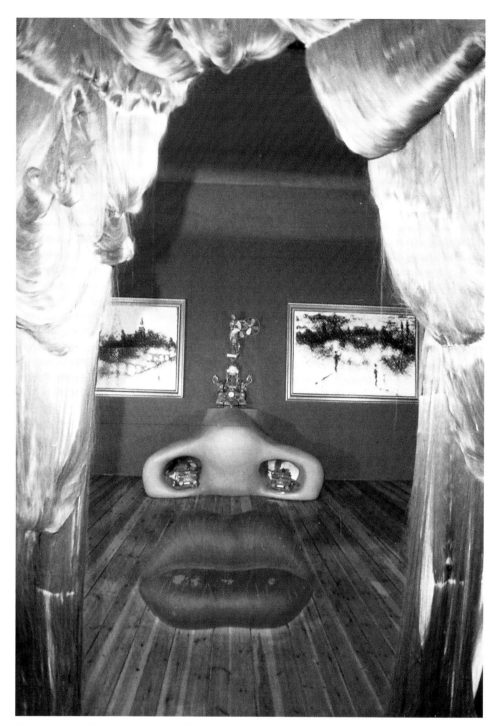

The face of Mae West by Salvador Dali (1934–6), Dali Museum, Figueras, Spain.

Even when good taste has insisted on reference to agreed forms, society has always allowed a certain eccentricity to flourish that is at variance with both order and good sense.

The 18th century Rococo movement at times became almost headache-inducing, notably in southern Italy, in Prague, and in Vienna. The ceilings of Tiepolo reflect its flour-

ishes, the secret meaning of which seems lost. Throughout the 19th century – a period of supreme eclecticism and one in which the arts systematically revisited earlier periods – eccentricity flourished through numerous personalities. They included all those who wanted to convey a sense in their interiors of the noxious Baudelairean perfumes of the *Fleurs du Mal*.

The English dandy Beau Brummell, it is said, bathed every morning in milk. Sometimes he took a whole hour to knot the fine cambric scarf round his neck to make his cravat. Meanwhile, his sovereign and admirer, the Prince Regent, later George IV, was building his extravagant Royal Pavilion at Brighton, that mix of Singhalese fairyland and

Left: "Snail" drawing room chair by Carlo Bugatti (1856–1940), Turin Exhibition, 1902 (Paris, Musée d'Orsay).
Right: The French actress Sarah Bernhardt (1844–1923) photographed at home.

Jean Cocteau compared modern art to fashion. He explained that whereas modern art produced things that were considered ugly before their beauty was understood, fashion did the reverse.

We must apply the same criteria to the attempts of today's small number of eccentrics. Their creations will only survive to the extent that they escape the vicissitudes of fashion.

From time to time it seems as if the angel of the bizarre passes over houses, leaving a contemporary element upon the styles he influences, and creating some remarkable, or at least remarked upon, landmarks.

Chinese mystery with its palm-tree-shaped columns and domes somewhat reminiscent of the Taj Mahal. Dandies did much to propagate eccentric style. "Simple pleasures," said the playwright and wit Oscar Wilde, "are the last refuge of the complex". One might reply with the symbolist poet Baudelaire's aphorism: "What is intoxicating in bad taste is the aristocratic pleasure of displeasing."

Robert de Montesquiou, a refined aesthete – one of those who inspired the novelist Marcel Proust – was to be one of the great promotors of the symbolist style. An admirer of the painter Gustave Moreau and of the poet Mallarmé, he supported artists of the Nancy school, the curved lines of Art Nouveau, and the vase-poems produced by that master in glass, Gallé.

Later on, the surrealists, enacting Lautréamont's definition – "As beautiful as a sewing machine meeting an umbrella on a dissection table" – would practice the art of collage and what was considered to be subversive media. It was Salvador Dali and the Giacometti brothers who influenced a whole decorative spirit. Within this sphere, the so-called "Neo-Romantic" painters, like Christian Bérard, would also exert their dictatorial influence on the taste of the day.

Automaton clock in varnished and gilded bronze, beginning of 19th century (former collection of Pascal Izarn).

Previous two pages
Three exceptional creations were made exclusively for David
Gill's loft by Garouste and Bonetti. On the left, a monumental
18-drawer sycamore chest of drawers with exterior finish in
white gold leaf. On the right, a Toledo multilamp, with resin
body and cuboid base, all in polished black, and lamp-brackets
in bronze gilt with cream silk shades.

Above and right
Karl Lagerfeld's apartment, designed as a pied-à-terre in 1995
on the 24th floor of the Roccabella residence in the principality
of Monaco. Furniture in blue-and-silver laquer by Ekart
Muthesius (Berlin, 1927) and coffee table by McArthur (1928).
The mirror screens are Karl Lagerfeld's design: Edifice sofa and
armchairs.

Above

Made in wood by the Venetian sculptor Livio de Marchi, this giant pot of brushes occupies an 18th century niche in the dining room of a Parisian apartment decorated by Stephanie Cauchoix. The two steel folding chairs are handmade following this designer's drawing: the seats are made of black-and-white hat straw.

Right

Isabella Gnecchi-Ruscone's home in Paris. On the Veronese mat-green lacquered walls are "Marilyn" silk-screen prints by Andy Warhol. The painted steel tea boxes are from the 19th century. The "Bokassa" (so-called) armchairs were discovered at the Marché aux Puces and covered in imitation panther: Lalique vase: Bouillotte Empire lamp.

Previous two pages
The walls of this library are lined
with built-in bookcases of polished oak:
on the shelves is a collection of Murano
vases dating from the 1950s. The two
armchairs and the desk, designed by
Elizabeth Garouste and Mattia Bonett
for Néotu, are of hammered iron covered
in cowskin. The matching floor-covering
is cowskin, placed on stripped coffee-
colored boards.

Left
André Dubreuil's reflection appears in
a large mirror which is decorated with
plates of hammered red leather: it is his
own design, and he closely monitored its
manufacture. In the foreground are a
pair of girandoles made of wrought iron
and crystal.

Right
Chest of drawers with three shaped
drawers covered entirely in canvas and
cotton cord: the frame and vase are in
the same material. There is a fragment
of marble column and an African statue.
All are by Christian Astuguevieille,
a Parisian designer and sculptor.

Left

In this bedroom at Aix-en-Provence, the furniture has been painted by the English-speaking artist Maxine de La Falaise. Fascinated by the colors and motifs of Africa, she has even painted the walls and beams. The "rabbit-eared" chair is covered in cotton from Niger; antique bed-covering from Morocco.

Above

The cane drawers of this kitchen unit contain table napkins and tablecloths. The old marble sink has taps discovered in a junk shop. The mosaic, designed by Maxine de La Falaise, is a mixture of shingle, stones, and pieces of Venetian glass obtained from Mosaïk.

In Maxime de La Falaise's
home, the large drawing
room, formerly a stable,
offers an eccentric mixture
of styles: African furniture
and beams painted by her;
Provençal influence in the
Stefanidis print covering
on the sofas (George
Smith); the "American
Empire" armchair in the
foreground, covered in
Ghanaian cotton fabric.

Above
The home of Charles Matton, painter and sculptor. An illusion
of size is created by a wardrobe with two mirrors, one untinted,
the other angled to create a *trompe-l'œil* effect. The 19th
century garden furniture sits round an octagonal kitchen table.

Right
Patchwork-style bathroom with differently patterned cement
tiles. The dog. Patch, sits in glory above the bathtub, which
was obtained from a demolition merchant in Bath. The
"Marguerite" chair to the left has an African-style covering.

Previous two pages
In Hong Kong, Mr Woo's bedroom was designed entirely
by Garouste and Bonetti. The room is an evocation of the
Chinoiserie elements that were fashionable in the 18th century:
the walls are hand-painted in pale gold; the bed-covering is of
satin silk with floral motifs that are seen also on the mat bronze
and gilt mushroom lamps; the animal-like coffee table is in
bronze and lacquer; a spare table is of bronze.

Left and above
Left, a pair of cabinets with snake-like motifs gouged cut, then
gilded. On the pedestal table sits a Pablo Picasso ceramic plate.
Above, the dining room has a three-tiered chandelier and a
table in mahogany; the central "Lazy Susan"-type tray in the
form of a soup tureen, supported by a foot in its axis, turns on
a bronze gilt hub. The walls are covered in old mirrors. The
frieze is by Gérard Garouste.

Above
A corner of the drawing room of couturier Olivier Guillemin.
The stuffed eagle was bought in Syria. The garden seat is in
cream laquered iron with leather seat and arms In the
foreground is an ecological chair made of recycled "Altuglas",
a creation of Olivier Védrine in the 1990s.

Right
The furniture Frédéric Molénac designs includes many
references to Africa, the continent where he spent his childhood.
Here this is reflected in the unfinished wood and the pairs of
horns. The table is made of a huge piece of exotic wood and
the legs comprise large interwoven horns.

*Provincial*style

Some people choose to get away from capital cities. But even in Paris it is possible to live in a style that is seemingly entirely French provincial. Many regard it as essential to have a "home sweet home", from where they can combat the disadvantages of city life by recreating the charm of times past, when our grandmothers embroidered their trousseaus by hand, the drawing-room clock set the pace of life, and the word "stress" was not known. The provincial style reflects a certain flair for living a modern life, while protecting oneself against today's frenetic pace by living in a setting that evokes a calm rural life.

The Château de l'Ange, a splendid 18th century residence on the borders of the Lubéron, has been fitted out by Édith Mézard, an embroidress, with the help of Michel Biehn, an antique dealer and interior decorator. The original door with its wrought-iron hinges remains. A painted metal "procession" lantern dominates.

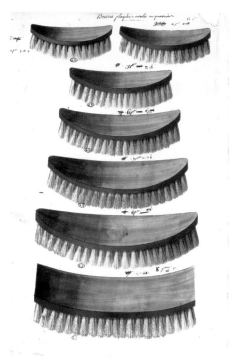

Designs for brushes, anonymous, First Empire period, France (Musée des Arts Décoratifs, Paris).

Hidden behind doors in Avignon are architectural marvels from the 17th and 18th centuries.

On the shelves of a convent library, there is an exceptional collection of "barbola" china.

One of the merits of the ongoing evolution in taste and color is that it reevaluates customs and items which were once generally regarded as undesirable. Suddenly, they have "charm", that vague yet pleasing description, something that is inexpressible but at the same time definitely there. That is precisely what, in this age of sprawling cities with their accompanying car madness, is conjured up by the provinces, which are now so much extolled for their good sense and, above all, their legendary art of living. A Parisian has only to meet someone from the country, and before he has opened his mouth the other man will

Alphonse Allais suggested rebuilding cities in the country. In the search for a certain quality of life, many city-dwellers are trying to make the opposite of this paradox a reality, through the discreet charms of interior decoration.

start boasting about this legendary quality of life that can only be found in the provinces. There is no need to leave the metropolis, however, in order to find places that are off the beaten track. Many people who live in the big city are determined to view it as just an agglomeration of villages. France may well be a centralized country, but most Parisians, or at least their parents, come from the countryside. Furthermore, quite a number of them still have a second home there.

Thanks to cast-offs from attics sold at auction, then restored or aged, depending on taste, a four-room flat in Paris can easily be turned into a country solicitor's residence. All it takes is a bit of silence (the provinces abhor noise), a tree over the roof, and some octagonal floor tiles. Add to that a strong whiff of polish; scatter around some bright, flowery cretonne fabrics; stuff an old-fashioned sideboard full of "home made jam" and a large Normandy-style wardrobe full of Provençal quilts. There you are right back to the good old days – the

height of comfort at a give-away price. Never since the introduction of electricity in blocks of flats and urban heating systems have so many candles and bundles of firewood been sold as in the last 20 years.

It is just a short step from the Clignancourt fleamarket to the market at l'Isle-sur-la-Sorgue in Provence. The younger generation made that step. Today they wind up

their grandfather clocks under the incredulous gaze of plausible ancestors framed in gold. Nothing stirs the emotions of the neo-provincials as much as genre scenes and still lifes by Jean-Baptiste Siméon Chardin, although this most Parisian of 18th-century painters rarely strayed from the banks of the Seine. The "country" now denotes something more than a region: it is a veritable state of mind.

Madeleine Castaing's home, the Maison de Lèves in the Eure valley. In the bedroom: the cast-iron swan's neck Directoire bed is padded with white satin; bedside table in rosewood and ivory (1830); early 19th century corner cupboard; bronze and biscuit lamps with biscuit bases (early 19th century); "Feuilletage" ("Foliage") wall fabric; "Nohan" carpet (Madeleine Castaing).

At Châteaurenaud. a huge 17th century residence in the Berry. Yves Halard has used daring color combinations from the period. while his wife has given free rein to her eclectic tastes in fabric.

Right
In the foreground of this view from drawing room to dining room. the wall coverings and curtains created by Lauer have been named after the property. The chairs are 18th century. and the rug on the parquet floor is an old kilim.

Below
The walls of this bathroom/living room are covered with a "Dame du Lac" ("Lady of the Lake") Liberty print by Lauer. The dressing table has been made from an old cutting table.

Left

Still at Châteaurenaud, in the blue bedroom, the wall coverings, curtains, and the canopy of the four-poster bed are in an "Aurélie" fabric (collection signed by Yves Halard for Lauer), which he has also used along the side of the bath. The bedspread is a quilt, also made by the owner of the house.

Above

This corner of the bedroom says everything about the gentle way of life in the country. It is an invitation to make the most of one's time in every room in the house. The pillow on the "Antonia" armchair is covered with an antique embroidered pillowcase.

Previous two pages
In their 18th century manor house in
Picardy, Anna and Gunther Lambert
have incorpoated a large number of
Liberty prints. Here in the bathroom
the wooden dado, painted in white
gloss, sets off the Liberty wall coverings.

Left
There is a profusion of styles in antique
dealer Jean-Pierre Rouayroux's 17th
century mansion in Montpellier. The
corridor walls are decorated in period
wallpaper, and the luxuriant garden
can be seen from the drawing room.

Above
Although Jean-Pierre Rouayroux likes
to juxtapose different styles, his favorite
periods are the late 18th and early
19th centuries. Here he has chosen
the Directoire style for the room that
he uses as his library.

Above
Jean-Pierre Rouayroux displays his passion for mixing styles in
his bedroom. On an Empire-style chest of drawers two lamps
frame travel souvenirs: corals brought back from Cuba, shells
from Tahiti, and a pair of Roman sphinxes.

Right
In this charming 17th century Montpellier mansion,
Louis XVI-style predominates in the living room painted in
blue-and-yellow monochrome. The carpet is Second Empire
and the cupboard Directoire style.

Previous two pages
Back to Châteaurenaud (pp. 64–7), the home of Yves and
Michelle Halard. The bathroom aptly displays the exceptional
amount of space given over to every room, a privilege that
is reserved for country houses. The gray tones of the wooden
floor match the color of the walls. The prints on the wall are
from Diderot's *Encyclopédie* (Encyclopedia).

Left
In his house at l'Isle-sur-la-Sorgue in Provence, antique
dealer-interior decorator Michel Biehn displays the fabrics
and objects that he collects and designs. A sofa covered in
silk serge, woven exclusively for him, sits imposingly in the
middle of the drawing room. The cotton cloth wall covering
was printed by Comoglio. Above the chimney is a painting
by David Oppenheim.

Above
From the past to the present, the city of Nîmes has always
managed to keep a real sense of *savoir faire*, as is shown by
these table accessories and appealing little gifts to be found
in Claude Bonnier's store, the Comptoir Gourmand.

Left

In their early 17th century residence, Dominique and Pierre Bénard-Dépalle preserved the austere atmosphere, while effectively introducing occasional extravagances. The kitchen, the simple style of which has been achieved with great care, is dominated by an 18th century Baroque chandelier in gilded wood.

Above

Rigor and whimsy are memorably combined in this home in the Périgord. The bedroom has a Louis XVI canopy bed and also a charming little gilded wooden chandelier with glass pendants. The bathroom is organized around a marble Empire bath, with a period floor in burnt terra-cotta tiles.

Previous two pages
Near Saint-Rémy-de-Provence, Bruno Lafourcade has skillfully
restored this beautiful 18th century country house in an eclectic
style which is both rigorous and imaginative. In the main
drawing room, the furniture and objects have been gleaned
from all over the world. The table has a made-to-measure top
which sits on old cabinet-maker's trestles. Two olive pots have
been used as bases for lamps. On the left is a sacristy chest.
The interior decoration is by Emile Garcin.

Above and right
Deep in the wilds of the Lubéron, decorator Anne-Marie de
Ganay has transformed a monastery into an elegant, sun-lit
home. The remains of the cloister have now become terraces
and pergolas, while the monks' cells (right) have been enlarged
and metamorphosed into bedrooms full of light and floral
decorations. The twin four-poster beds are made of painted
wood and covered with flowery cretonne.

Seeking tranquility, but
also comfort, Terry and
Jean de Gunzburg asked
interior decorator Jacques
Grange to rethink this
Provençal farmhouse.
Together, they designed a
large kitchen where meals
can be eaten in winter. The
open cupboards, which
give a glimpse of the
collections of colored
glasses and plates inside,
were created by
reassembling 19th century
pine doors from bistros.
The central light is by
Claude Lalanne; 1940s
oak table; 1920s
gloss-painted wooden
chairs by Thonet.

*Atlantic*style

The deep blue sea, with a touch of white on the crest of the waves, appealingly offsets the painted clapboard cabins – with what look like hat veils on their gabled roofs but are in fact fishing nets – and serve as a reminder that on the Atlantic coast of France everything is dictated by the ocean. Squalls, fish creels, shrimping nets, and sea salt. This is the bracing open-air life! The cool sea spray, the subtle flavors you can expect from fish, the table of high and low tides, the tonic effect of the great family swimming expeditions or bike rides. Many ocean lovers live on the islands, but even those who live on the coast seem to be islanders in their hearts.

A simple, refined style, in a village house on the Ile de Ré, in Ars-en-Ré.
This staircase effect sums up the decorative spirit of the house. The interior has been completely covered with panels glossed in ivory white, both for aesthetic effect and to protect against the ever-present salt.

Above: An old fisherman's lifebelt.
Top: the *Britannia* sailing ship, summer 1913
(Beken of Cowes, Sea & See collection).

The ocean, its salt, and its traditions make it essential to decorate houses here in a way that is in keeping with the demands of a highly specialized climate and way of living. When you live by the sea, there is obviously going to be an interaction between inside and outside which cannot be avoided. Every house on the Atlantic is a boat at anchor in its own right.

The west coast of France is less hospitable but better protected than the shores of the Mediterranean. Atlantic or Riviera? This age-old choice divides France in two, between on the one hand, the luxury of the

A model ship in a bottle (early 20th century).

spring tides, and on the other, the delights of relaxing on the beach.

If there is a western style *par excellence*, in France it must be the one to be found on the coast that represents the last stop before the great ocean crossing. You would think it was only a short swim from Long Island to the Ile de Ré, given how squarely their houses face each other across the expanse and how similar they are. The same brightly glossed clapboards, the same horizons stretching away to infinity, the same sound of the waves blotting out any other noise, the same happy feeling of being free and alone with the ocean.

Atlantic houses generally appear fragile and are kept meticulously scrubbed. The slightest sign of rust is hunted down. Here the salt eats away at everything, except when the house is made of granite, a mineral that is grayer than the sky on a stormy day.

Above: A presbytery built in Brittany granite, between Guingamp and Lannion.
Below left: An old shop sign in painted wrought iron, Saint-Malo.

No doubt it is because the environment around coastal houses can be hostile that the people here cultivate an atmosphere of hospitality, warmth, and solidarity, and perhaps value it more highly than elsewhere. As they enjoy a meal of fresh fish, steamed or cooked in sea salt, there is a sense of friendship and modesty that is imposed by the elements.

Everyone wants to be thought of as something of a fisherman on these happy islands, which fiercely defend their individuality and struggle more courageously than other areas against modern-day pollution.

Canvas and linen, gloss paint and limewash, rubber pointing, and large garbage cans to swallow up all the shells from those delicious shellfish. Bistros with low ceilings where people sing even more than they drink. Backs bent by a sudden gust of wind. And then those boards surfing on the waves, the pink color of shrimps, the mauve shade of blue hydrangeas, the creaking of shop signs, the memory of smugglers: so many seaside dreams. And as well as that, one lesson that is omnipresent: respect for nature is never too much to ask.

Previous two pages
At Loix on the Ile de Ré, interior architect Christian Liaigre has his own interpretation of the Atlantic style. The exceedingly clean, pure feel of the all-white dining room provides an excellent setting for the furniture he has designed. In the foreground a large table. On the wall he has devised a clever way to hang pictures and various other objects.

Above
A bedroom with a monastic spirit, where the heads of the twin oak beds, designed by Liaigre, have been woven in straw collected in the Vendée marshes and are offset by ivory linen sheets. Here is a good idea for a damp climate: the upper part of a closet door is openwork so that the air can circulate inside.

Right
Still on Ré, but in the village of Saint-Martin, architect A. Blanchet has managed to combine the local style with that of the east coast of the United States. The summer bathroom is organized around two washbasins inserted into an old workbench. The wooden bath is hooped with metal, like a barrel.

Left, top

This Christian Liaigre living room displays a harmony of subtle shades of white, from the armchair covers and the chalky stone of the Saintonge fireplace to the ivory whites of the corals brought back from Bora Bora. A wooden screen with adjustable slats, similar to those used in the Caribbean, cuts the room off from the street.

Left, bottom

This bedroom in a village house in Portes-aux-Rés is separated from the bathroom by a screen door with another one next to it which opens onto the dressing room. An English pine corner cupboard is a feature in the bathroom. In the foreground the two straw chairs were woven by Jean-Michel Frank. The Indian carpet is from David Hicks.

Right

For his house in Loix, Christian Liaigre designed a glassed-in area for storing raincoats, boots, and even a bicycle – an indispensable accessory on the island. Coral red is the only strong color in the house, making it a particularly striking aspect of the decor.

Previous two pages

In Christian Liaigre's living room at Ré, light floods through the large square-paned picture window. The pine-paneled walls are painted matte white, and contrast strongly with the armchairs in blackened beechwood with thick black leather seats. On the light oak floor is a woven Thai carpet. The "Opium" bed is covered in a grayish-green linen fabric.

Above

It is most pleasing to drink a glass of white wine in the shade of the fig tree in this small courtyard, which is designed as a real open-air room: an ideal place to take advantage of the exceptional light in the Ile de Ré. The steel chairs are by Michel Aragon.

Right

Lightness and solidity combine in this New England-style bedroom-bathroom, where an American patchwork quilt warmly covers a canopy bed. The striking floor of the room is of reconstituted stone. There is a "Bertoia" sink unit by Knoll and a sisal carpet (Casa Lopez).

Previous two pages
In 1985 Alain and Annick Goutal fitted
out this living room, which is bathed in
light from a window opening onto the
garden. The junk shop armchairs were
covered in fabric to suit the room. The
painting is by Harrisson (19th century):
Art Deco lamp.

Left
Features of this kitchen and dining room
include a table top unusually supported
by a 1930s lamp post base. There is
an English pine cupboard and wrought-
iron seats that are copies of 18th century
models. Billiard-table lights add a
special touch to the room.

Above
The walls of this living room are entirely
covered in light pine. There is a long
view over the garden from the studio-
style window. Various objects on the
windowsill were picked up in the local
fleamarkets. The turned wooden chairs
are by Thonet.

Following two pages
The fireplace in this living room
is recessed between fitted wooden
cupboards; above the mantlepiece is a
19th century painting of the sea, and in
the foreground is a Thonet *chaise longue*
(Stéphane Deschamps). The floor is of
speckled sandstone tiles.

*Provence*style

The sun is an obsession with people today, and it is the sun that persuades many of the French living north of the Loire to periodically migrate south to Provence, a region in southeast France. Below Montélimar, where people's accents start to lilt and cicadas chirp, a whole region is transformed. Provence has its own peculiarities, flavors, and colors – all of which are discernible in recent decorative trends. What is generally regarded as being "Provençal" actually comprises a wonderfully large diversity of landscapes and styles, from the patrician charm of villas in Aix to shepherds' huts, from the ridge of the Alpilles to the seaboard of the Mediterranean.

In this town house, an appealing kind of cool cave has been created in a corner of the courtyard. Tha Moroccan-inspired pool is equipped to facilitate bathing, or even swimming, in this special private setting.

A variant of French Provincial style. "Provençal" style consists of the free interpretation – mainly by people from elsewhere – of traditions special to the South of France; or, to be more precise, the eastern part of France south of Montélimar. There, it seems, the sun endows even the humblest of objects with a special something. Think of the markets of Provence: the pyramids of egg plants (aubergines), the chair upholsterers, the sellers of bric-à-brac, or the scents of spices. Van Gogh, Cézanne, Matisse, along with so many less prestigious painters, have passed through here. They have

taught the people of the north to look upon this pebbled land with so special an eye that even the smallest stone pile here may cost a fortune.

This pastoral symphony did not start yesterday. Long ago Alphonse Daudet interested his contemporaries in Provençal windmills. The mill at Fontvieille, in which he never lived but in whose shade legend will have it he wrote, is today one of the most unauthentic, yet most visited buildings in France.

Thus, since the 19th century, in successive waves, newcomers have continued to discover and relish the

A lead fountain, 17th century, Arles.

T radition has remained more alive in Provence than anywhere else in France, shining like a sun and drawing to the song of its cicadas appreciative citizens and visitors from all over the world.

charms of Provence. Such praises were sung convincingly by Frédéric Mistral, Marcel Pagnol, Fernandel, Souleiado, and Christian Lacroix: from the arid charm of the sheepfolds to the pottery courses, from the chant of the cicadas to the vivid patterns on the calicoes that come to us, via the port of Marseille, from faraway Asia.

Blends of tones that would seem unthinkable north of Lyon suddenly make sense in the delta of the Rhône. All the great civilizations, from the Greeks to the Iberians, have been through here, and Roman Gaul made Arles one of its capitals. The river, navigable as far as Lyon, brought goods from the industries of the

Far left: In Michael Biehn's home on the Isle-sur-la-Sorgue, a Provençal wardrobe containing *boutis*, printed calicoes, indigoes, silk piqués, and old cottons.
Left: An 1880 moiré dress, and cashmere woven at Nîmes *c.* 1840. Musée du vieux Nîmes, Place aux Herbes.

Nordic regions, which would cross the path of those newly docking from the east.

Located at the crossroads of two ways of speech, Provençal is not a dialect but a language that is still both written and spoken. Few French provinces have so vibrant a local tradition as does Provence.

As for the horizons of Provence, where would you find such a variety of landscapes so close together? The marshlands of the Camargue or the Chaîne du Lubéron, the noble countryside of Aix, the ridges of the Alpilles, the wilderness of Crau, or the Salins du Midi. Similarly, in Provence the realm of interior decoration sings and changes like the Provençal accent known the world over.

Above: Sewing workshop, Arles, *c.* 1785, by Antoine Raspal (Collection Musée Réattu, Arles).
Left: Place de la République, Arles, *c.* 1900.

109

In a patrician residence
in the ancient city of
Arles, the drawing-room
walls are covered with
trompe-l'oeil canvases,
which give the impression
of being drawings; they
are attributed to the local
painter Réatu. This is a
decor of Neoclassical
inspiration: a pair of
plaster busts, patinated
terra-cotta-style, sit on
their pedestals, one on
either side of the French
doors.

Provence style

Above

An imposing collection of earthenware (Véronique Pichon, Uzès) is reflected in an engraved Venetian-origin mirror. Glimpsed also is a bouquet of candles (Gilbert Jean), and there is a wrought-iron chandelier (Vicent Mit l'Âne.

Right

The entrance to a *bastide*, a fortified county house, in the Uzès district. The 18th-century wrought-iron balustrade runs up three floors. The wrought-iron armchairs follow a design by Hervé Baume: varnished earthenware jars are of Spanish origin.

112

Left
Edith Mézard's Tuscan-style home in the
Lubéron. A pathway of recently planted
cypresses emphasizes the architectural
severity of the garden façade of the
Château de l'Ange.

Right
The garden of this house near
Saint-Rémy-de-Provence features beds
of Italian and Portuguese boxwood.
There are rambler roses round the door,
box and other plants in "Anduze" pots
in the foreground. The façade was
restored by Bruno Lafourcade.

Above
Bohemian chic is expressed in Irène and
Giorgio Silvagni's guest bedroom. Above
the Empire bed, a giant mosquito net
has been fitted out with an abundance
of Indian cotton. On the right is a 1940s
table and, in the foreground, Provençal
piqué fabric bought in the Tarascon
fleamarket.

Right
In the Silvagnis' home, the double
"Pallière" doors open onto the master
bedroom, revealing a bookcase-cupboard
with grating and incorporated desk
features. The woven leather armchairs
are by Mies van der Rohe. Also seen
is a 1940s wrought-iron chandelier and
a Moroccan carpet.

Following two pages
In front of Jacques Grange's country
house at Saint-Rémy-de-Provence, the
wisteria-shaded terraces become an
outside dining area thoughout the
summer. Set in the midst of vegetation,
this house with traditional lime-rendered
walls is charmingly enhanced by the
garden designed by Monsieur Semini.

Previous two pages
A typical Provençal kitchen, adapted for eating, in an extremely old *bastide*, or fortified, house. The rustic furniture is covered in a local cotton fabric. The "chandeliers" are baskets of dried aromatic plants. The fleamarkets of the region have furnished most of the objects in this decor of refined simplicity.

Above
The discreet charm of the Provençal bourgoisie is exhibited in this combined drawing room and library. The 18th century furniture is in the spirit of the Musée Calvet at Avignon. The walls have been patinated by Francesca Bredin-Hobart. The candlesticks with metal shades were imported from the USA.

Right
In the home of Maxime de La Falaise, the round table has an imitation marble-painted top and dragon legs; above the table is a old Turkish lamp. On the mantle shelf over the fireplace are 1940s flower-pot holders of molded cement as well as an African mask. The chairs were painted by Maxime.

Previous two pages

This garden designed by Dominique Lafourcade in the environs of Saint-Rémy-de-Provence has created a verdant "drawing room". Meals are taken in front of the house by the large pool, the coolness of which is appreciated in summer.

Above

The home of the antique dealer and interior decorator Michel Biehn at Isle-sur-la-Sorgue. Two reversible *boutis* of 19th-century pigeon-breast silk are nonchalantly placed on a gilded wooden sofa dating from the 1940s, which is covered in gray-brown linen.

Right

At a home in Nîmes, there is a clash of styles with a group comprising a stone sphynx, an Empire metal lamp, and a frame decorated with seashells, all seen against a Provençal fresco. The lamp and mirror have been placed on a sofa painted in the regional Provençal style.

*Chalet*style

A mountain remains one of 20th century urban man's greatest conquests. And to own a chalet in the mountains is one of his greatest luxuries. More than any other home, a chalet is built to reassure and protect. Its enemy — the cold — is ardently beaten back by wood, and not simply by the wood that is burned on the hearth, but also by the fine fir trees that form the basis of any structure erected on the steep and snowy slopes. Nowhere do notions of comfort, warmth, nestling, and good company count for more than in a chalet in the mountains, by the sea or even in a garden.

The entrance hall to the Mont Blanc chalet-hotel is decorated with a stag's head, beneath which an old chest of Tarentaise origin bears a pair of 19th century candlesticks, and a basket of apples and pinecones; the clock is from Franche-Comté.

A balcony of the Lodge Park hotel overlooks the small village of Megève: Artesania chair; Ralph Lauren plaid; a small Flamant basket.

For lovers of winter sports, the chalet is first and foremost a warm place to sleep before donning skis and going "up the mountain". But well before such dangerous outdoor activities became popular, the chalet idea had already seduced the romantics. And it wasn't confined to the mountains either. You find chalets all over Europe: by the sea, in the country, in parks and gardens. They are built either for fanciful or essential reasons. Wood is the main element, both in terms of the structure and its decoration. Most chalets are constructed either for leisure activities or as back-up accommodation.

Switzerland is the place where the chalet developed and gained importance as a space for living. Here the walls are traditionally made out of tree trunks or squared-off beams placed on top of one another. Or it may be a permanent structure clad with planks of wood and sporting open balconies.

Whatever the method, wood is the key material. And not just any wood. This is pine, the "Christmas tree", with all its emotive symbolism. It is this that creates the chalet's special atmosphere of warmth, well-being, and penetrating scents, the impression of being within an immense violin or cigar box. Plus that other function of wood, the burning of it in the hearth. For the fireplace is the central focus of any stay in the mountains. It is all part of the unrefined lifestyle, even if in today's terms it most often embodies a city-dweller's luxury.

The chalet, the "home sweet home" of mountain folk, has never worried itself about including excesses of sentimentalized decoration. What might be considered unbearable elsewhere seems in this setting to be perfectly charming. Colorful and scented geraniums often play an essential decorative role, evoking a balancing feminine presence in this masculine world of woodcutters and mountain climbers. From the good inn of the Cheval Blanc to the vintage futurism of Avoriaz, from Tyrolian singers to top sportsmen, from shepherds to tanned visitors, the chalet remains one of those human dwellings that have most in common with the cave of prehistory. It embodies and offers a way of returning to humanity's roots; its primitivism, like its decoration, represents a taming of nature. Is not the chalet a perfect country home?

The wood of which the traditional chalet is built endows this form of country house with its very special warm and comforting character. Of all building types, this is one that happily puts city-dwellers back in touch with their primitive origins.

Top: The life of hunters is evoked by this imitation staghorn Flamant electric light fitting.

Far left: A poster by Abel Faivre publicizes winter sports at Chamonix and advertises railroad services from Paris to Lyon and the Mediterranean.

Left: In a chalet at Gstaad, tea is served in the small drawing room on a huge fir stump. The divan is covered in imitation fur (Wilderness).

Previous two pages
The sophisticated simplicity of a house near Klosters. The corner terrace, partly covered and protected from the wind, is decorated with hunting trophies.

Above
A 19th century crystal chandelier lights this chalet's stairwell with its pleasing perforated paneling that is so typical of Swiss chalets.

Right
An effective contrast has been created by placing the Venetian mirror on the rough wood of this bedroom; the objects were mostly bargains from fleamarkets.

Previous two pages

The lounge in the Mont Blanc hotel has a particularly warm feel with its comfortable armchairs covered in a plain check (Nobilis). The pine and oak furniture goes with the ancient woodwork. The boxes are made out of bark (SIA), and the old frames were purchased from Esprit de Charme.

Above

On the Baroque-style saloon console stands a collection of different-shaped photophores (candle holders with glass shades). Between the two windows is an abstract painting by Martin Disler. On the right-hand side is a Baroque wall lamp which was bought at the Marché aux Puces.

Opposite

This comfortable-looking canopy bed was made by a local craftsman to the owner's specification. Stag and ibex antlers decorate the whole room. In the foreground is a smooth leather armchair. The bedspread is by Agnès Comar.

Previous two pages
In the upstairs drawing-room of this
chalet in Megève over 1.000 square feet
perfectly display its 18th century roof-
structure. The metal coffee table in the
foreground was designed by Michèle
Rédélé and made by Monsieur Grosset,
a local craftsman in ironwork. The sofa
is covered in a "drap de Bonneval"
(Nouilhac).

Above
In this chalet at Chamonix, dating from
1900, the drawing room is heated by a
chimney stove, decorated with two small
copper balls in a late 18th century style
(Godin). The plaid and the wooden
basket come from David Hicks. In the
foreground is a Charles Eames armchair.
The table of Chamonix granite was
designed by the owner; a Mexican carpet.

Right
In this drawing room. built of tree
trunks left in their raw state. the sofas
and pouffes are covered in a taupe
woolen material (Canovas). The console.
iron table, glasses, and lamps come
from First Time. The staircase, also
constructed of tree trunks, leads to the
owners' bedroom and to the mezzanine.
which has been converted into an office.

Chalet style

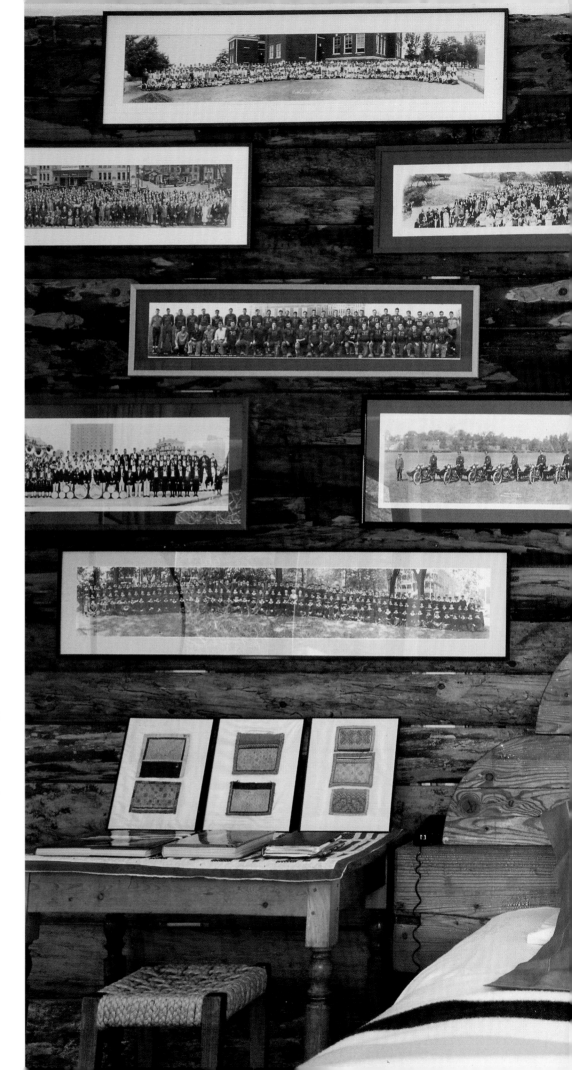

Right
A fine collection of very early 20th century group photos (football teams, universities, colleges) adorns the raw plank walls of this bedroom. The recess at the head of the bed contains an old Pontiac sign depicting an American Indian in profile. To the right is a Hermès shopping bag.

Following two pages
Luxuriously functional, this bathroom's pine woodwork houses a bathtub, washbasin, and drawers. The heated towel-rail is by Czech & Speak; linen by Catherine Memmi; taps from DornBrach.

Previous two pages
Wood in a patchwork style
lies at the heart of this
warm and lively Chamonix
chalet. Here are two views
of the paneled entrance
hall with its collection of
American plates and old
photographs.
On the left is an African
armchair of the 1950s.
The bookshelves make use
of concrete blocks.
On the right is an
American sled together
with a pair of wood-and-
string armchairs.

Right
Pine boards create a
canopy effect in this
bedroom with bathroom,
enhanced by a magnificent
English ship's chest
(Village Suisse). The
armchair by First Time is
covered in Alcantara
(Lelièvre); Persian carpet
and canvas blinds (Casal);
bed and bath linen (Olivier
Desforges); bed end wall
lights (Manufactor).

*Eclectic*style

Hoarding and accumulation, ethics and mannerisms, the love of bric-à-brac, curiosity seen as the nicest of faults. Since the 19th century such behavior seems to have been the rule among those who are fortunate. How they excel in the art of mixing and matching! The great developments in tourism, the recurrent interest in the exotic and historic, the art of pastiche carried to the point of kitsch – all have contributed greatly to the current enthusiasm for eclecticism. It's a development all the more remarkable inasmuch as it encapsulates a whole century of elegance and the art of living off the beaten track.

A grotto armchair (Venice, 18th century), a portrait by Duncan Grant (England, 1915), and a seashell console (neo-Regency, *c.* 1935) mingle with objects gleaned by the illustrator Pierre Le Tan from salerooms over the last 20 years.

An optical effect at the Château de Groussay. A witch's mirror reflects the composite decor of the famous library conceived along English lines by Carlos de Besteguy in the 1940s.

When after World War Two, the famous shoemaker Roger Vivier boldly placed African statuettes on the Boulle furniture in his splendid residence, people were shocked. When his contemporaries of the 1950s and 1960s followed his example, mixing Knoll seating with Tiffany lamps, and English furniture with abstract paintings, many voices protested.

Even so, this wasn't the first time that eclectic style had appeared. By the end of the 18th century, there was a tendency, particularly in England, to break resolutely with the idea of the "grand ensemble" so typical of the Age of Enlightenment in Europe and the French Ancien Régime. The important factor behind this deliberately organized disorder was travel.

and particularly by the wealthy young from the English side of the Channel. Versailles and its gardens, Paris and the most clever of its enlightened salons, then the Swiss Alps (including, if possible, a pilgrimage to Fernay, to Voltaire's bedside), later (in the footsteps of Stendhal), the slow descent of the "boot" of Italy, Milan and La Scala, the open city of Rome, Naples, Pompeii, and right into Sicily. They called it the "Grand Tour". When they returned home, their bags were full of treasures. Copies of antiquities,

drawings, and porcelains were the equivalents in those days of our souvenirs. On his return to the foggy north, the young aristocrat would thenceforth settle for the rest of his life to the pleasures of hunting and marriage. Yet he was able to continue to dream, surrounded by the objects he had gathered on his travels, from the lands where it never rains.

Simultaneously developing a passion for the medieval and a leaning towards orientalism, romanticism was to deepen this eclecticism. Burgeoning

industries would adapt it to the needs and means of a whole new bourgeoisie. It was henceforth left to the official salons, the reception rooms, and the odd lover of the grand style to go in for and still enjoy the *ensemble*. But in less formal surroundings, tastes were multiplying in favor of the accumulation of, and unexpected union of, objects that no one could have previously foreseen would one day come together in such a stimulating way.

Close relations existed between the upper classes throughout Europe, and presents were sent from one country to another, mixing the folklore of the two – from Balmoral to Capodimonte, from the boudoir of a grand duchess to the residence of a Portuguese royal highness. In the present, the enjoyment of sentimental disorder continues in the eclectic style to which those who are most expert in the art add their own very personal touch.

Having roamed around, and borrowed successively from all styles and countries from the 19th century onward, Europeans have evolved a tasteful eclecticism. In this society, self-recognition is essentially created through difference and maintaining distance from everyday realities.

Below: Painted in the 1950s in the style of the 19th century, two watercolors by Serebriakoff depict the vestibule and a guest room at Groussay.

Previous two pages

A gallery runs the length of this splendid Basque house in
Biarritz, where periods and styles do not clash. There is an oak
parquet floor, and walls are hung with a Hamot floral percale.
The dining room contains Louis XVI seats, a Baguès chandelier,
and Roux-Spitz standard-lamps (*c.* 1925). In the gallery there
is a Thonet *chaise longue*, small white armchairs by Francis
Jourdain; a Sauvage desk; and a lovely "Majorelle" piece.

Left and above

These twin Italian beds are decorated with allegorical sculptures
of Fortune and Sleep. On the wall is a lithography by Picasso
and a medley of drawings by Edouard Detaille (19th century).
Above, in the winter garden in southwestern France, the
foreground contains a sofa and a tea table by Thonet and a pair
of cane armchairs (1920s).

Previous two pages
Two painted and glazed
metal pavilions, by the
interior designer François-
Joseph Graff, sit in the
seclusion of a hollowed-out
garden, laid out by Pierre
Bergé, not far from the
Seine. One pavilion, seen
here, is used as an office, in
which there is a Regency
piece in green lacquer, a
chintz-covered 19th
century armchair, and
copper reading lamps with
green silk shades.
Landscaping by Pascal
Cribier.

Opposite
In the stylist Gilles
Dufour's home, the main
bedroom features his
portrait in silhouette by
Karl Lagerfeld hanging
over a large bed. The bed
is lined with material from
Prud'homme and covered
by an Amish quilt. The
lamp and shade were made
following a design by
Garouste and Bonetti. The
end wall, painted to create
the impression that it is
larger, is decorated with
cut-out silhouettes and
English engravings
(Bennison).

Above

In this entrance hall, which has been converted into an office
by Gilles Dufour, stands a Provençal desk with a large romantic
mirror hanging above it; placed on the center top of the desk is
a symbolist period mask by Ringel Del Zaahr.

Right

Detail of the above. Gilles Dufour has enhanced this
19th century painted iron wall light by adding colored-glass
candle rings unearthed at the Marché des Puces and a dried
starfish, treated by the stylist with mercurochrome.

Previous two pages
Left: Sculpted woodwork
painted in imitation wood
with gilded moldings.
Fine 18th century books
rub shoulders in this
multi-style drawing room
with a collection of
pictures closely hung
together. There is a
Pierre Chareau 1930s
cane armchair, and a tub
easy chair, 19th century.
Right: Another view of the
drawing room. Between
the tall windows is a
simple console from
Habitat, and on it bronze
Syrian candlesticks. On
the pedestal is a terra-
cotta Revolutionary Period
bust; parquet flooring of
the Versailles type.

Left
Cross-fertilization of
eras and styles in a 17th
century private mansion
in Paris. On the 1940s
carpet, the 1930s furniture
is covered in emerald-
green silk velour. There is
a Dunan vase and a rare
African Kota reliquary in
wood and studded copper.
The mantelpiece area and
its mirror background are
decorated with pictures
and cubist works by
Miklos. The low table is by
Jean-Michel Frank; Sornay
1930s sofa and armchairs.

169

Left

The lively colors in the drawing room of this 17th century mansion encompass a 1930s sofa covered in emerald-green velour. A wooden African antelope has been placed against a background of mauve anemones (Marianne Robic); Le Gall and Bérard paintings; "Cocteau"-inspired plaster chandelier; 1940s carpet.

Above

On a Jansen chest of drawers painted in carnival-style (1945), the valuer Rémy Le Fur has placed a selection of African masks and statuettes along with an Egyptian head. Above them hangs a large oil painting by Christian Bérard, which is entitled "Man in actor's costume".

Previous two pages
In the dressing-room extension to his
bathroom. Hubert Le Gall has cleverly
covered the glazed closet doors with old
Moroccan photographs from an album
bought in the Drouot-Paris saleroom.
The armchairs are of Asiatic origin.

Above and right
The Parisian loft of Pierre Passebon.
There is contrast between a neo-Gothic
piece and cartoon-strip original plates.
Opposite right is an invitation to go
traveling. The woodwork is 18th-century

Syrian. erected only a stone's throw from
the Bastille. On the wall are two works
on kraft paper by Bob Elia. A large
(36 x 20 ft) Indian carpet and two
fulsome cushions in a Moroccan fabric
are on the floor.

Previous two pages

In her artist's studio the interior decorator Florence Lopez of the Rue du Dragon has succeeded in harmonizing some rare old photographs of ancient Rome (Cuccioni, 1857), a desk designed by George Nelson (USA, 1960s), laboratory glassware, and a rare chromium medical lamp. On the studded leather sofa (England, 19th century) is a silk Japanese stole and a model armchair from Herman Miller's studio.

Above and right

In the office of interior architect Tino Zezvudacchi, a large beveled mirror that he designed dominates a desk and modernist seating in leather and chrome tubing (Pel's, England, 1930s). The carpet was also designed by him, and it was produced by the Diurne gallery. On the right, the small drawing room, hung with green cloth, brings together 19th century orientalist illustrations. The 19th century carpet is Persian.

Six Parisian fashion designers *at home*

Paris has its fashion houses with their seasonal creations. Yet the decorative arts cannot be split off from those of *haute couture*, for they are no less intimate extensions of the human physique and personality. Most fashion designers of recent history have taken as much care with the design of their professional and private spaces as they have with their fashion designs. After all, the one is the context in which the others are created. Similarly, the great fashion labels of today are extending the stylistic particularities of their individual creators into many other lifestyle areas. Such interchange is as alive now as it was in the past and provides excellent insight into the sensitivities and tastes of the times.

The large drawing room in Yves Saint-Laurent's Paris residence: the designer and his model. On the wall is an important canvas by Fernand Léger. In the foreground. on a Chinese lacquer table sit Italian Renaissance bronzes and various 16th and 17th century curiosities: rock crystal globe.

"Men who have taste", fashion designers, stylists and interior designers, all occupy a similar place in the hearts and preoccupations of their female clients. Rare are those women who do not attune their attire to the environment in which they live. In a similar manner, the commercial premises and residences of the creators of fashion reflect, albeit indirectly, the particularities of their work. Additionally, many of the masters of *couture* are often themselves remarkable collectors.

The example was set long ago, and was a lofty one: Jacques Doucet (1853–1929). Though Doucet did not revolutionize the world by the originality of his fashion designs, his reputation persists, more than 70 years after his death, as one of the prime collectors of our time. At the turn of the 19th century, he was one of the few Frenchmen to pave the way from the classic taste embodied by Louis XV and Louis XVI furniture, artistic objects, and paintings on the one hand, to modern artistic expressions on the other. He progressively sold the former in order to acquire the latter. His collection ranged from the post impressionists via the arts of Asia and Africa and the cubists, to Marcel Duchamp and the surrealists. His pupil Paul Poiret pushed things further forward still. In addition to launching a fashion house, he started a studio, "Martine", intended to create new textiles, furniture, and decorative objects. Though the enterprise lacked permanence, it enjoyed a certain success during the 1920s. It also blazed a trail, which today's great fashion labels have followed by

"Chez Poiret" models, illustrated by G. Barbier. (Musée de la Mode et du Costume, Palais Galliera)

Above: Jacques Doucet's studio at Neuilly in 1929. On the wall, "La Charmeuse de Serpents" by Henri Rousseau, "le Douanier". Hung close together are works by Picasso, Chirico, Cézanne, and others; sofa by Couard; Lalique flecked glass doors.
Right: Mademoiselle Chanel's reception room at 31 Rue Cambon, Paris, containing a coromandel laquer screen and 18th century gilded wood.

extending the range of products claiming the prestige of their name. Thus, Giorgio Armani has just launched a line of furniture and decorative accessories. And Christian Dior, too, has always had an immensely important interior decoration side.

As a client and friend of Albert Rateau, a master of Art Deco, the fashion designer Jeanne Lanvin entrusted him between the wars with refitting her private mansion, her fashion house in the Rue du Faubourg Saint-Honoré, then her menswear shop, which is still opposite, and finally a store that sold things for the home, the interior designer of which was also briefly the artistic director until his untimely death. Then there was the intimate relationship between the eccentric Elsa Schiaparelli and Jean-Michel Frank, the interior designer of her shop and the salons where she worked in the Place Vendôme. And her friendship for such artists as Salvador Dali, Christian Bérard, and Jean Cocteau, with whom she was associated in her creative activity. The apartment of Coco Chanel, above her salons in the Rue Cambon, remains unchanged, a perfect example of taste. As for Christian Dior himself, as talented in the planning of a decor as in designing a dress, he was able to resurrect the Louis XVI style of 1900 in the early 1950s: Medallion armchairs, gray and white stripes, Neoclassical woodwork. A style which became an emblem of his business. Forty years later, Christian Lacroix would advance the phenomenon even further: in order to decorate the premises he would open in 1997, he took on two talents of his own generation, as unknown then as he was himself: Elisabeth Garouste and Mattia Bonetti. The success Lacroix enjoyed was inseparable from his art and style.

And so the old story carries on, that of the love between fashion and decor, which has lasted for more than 150 years. There is little doubt that its ongoing history continues to hold in store for us many more pleasant surprises.

For over a hundred years, the points of contact between the fashion world and that of interior design have multiplied. The truth of this interchange is clearly to be seen in the homes of fashion creators, whose immediate environments are explicit reflections of their work.

Left: Jeanne Lanvin's bedroom, decorated by Armand-Albert Rateau between 1920 and 1922. The walls in Lanvin blue silk are embroidered with marguerites, white daisies, using silver thread, evoking Jeanne's much loved daughter's name.

Left
The terrace of the summer pavilion at the Villa Oasis at Marrakech, the oriental dream imagined by Majorelle: bright blue balustrades; pale rose color wall rendering. Here is where Yves Saint Laurent relaxes after each *haute couture* collection.

Right
The "Menzeh", the most informal room in which to relax at the Villa Oasis: cord armchairs (1940s) mingle with Art Deco furniture, such as the desk made for the fashion designer Madeleine Vionnet; large Moroccan lantern (early 20th century); bamboo style table (1900). The view overlooks the garden and pond designed by Majorelle in the 1920s.

Yves Saint Laurent

Born on the southern side of the Mediterranean, this most prestigious of French fashion designers has forgotten nothing of his origins or of French colonization. In the very heart of Marrakech he has created, with incredible luxury, the sort of dream residence that mixes the influence of the Orient with the exotic side of European taste. In this, Saint Laurent is continuing a tradition. The villa and surrounding gardens were originally created by the painter Majorelle, whose palette in the 1920s revealed to the west the fairyland character of this colorful countryside at the foot of the Atlas Mountains.

Previous two pages

"Luxury, calm, and sensuousness": the terrace adjoining the "Menzeh", constructed in 1924 to a half modern, half oriental design conceived by the painter Majorelle, son of the famous Art Nouveau cabinet maker. Aided by the architect Bill Willis and interior designer Jacques Grange, Yves Saint Laurent has today entirely refurbished it. Part of the extraordinary garden is open to the public.

Above, left

A corner of Yves Saint Laurent's bedroom: Syrian furniture inlaid with mother of pearl, and Anglo-Indian armchair; French crystal chandelier (18th century).

Above, right

The desk placed at an angle to the window enables the fashion designer to draw, making use of the best light and the view over the garden bamboos; Arts and Crafts furniture.

Right

A palette of blues and pale greens inspired by Henri Matisse graces this drawing room; Anglo-Indian sofa upholstered in braided gold; Romantic period pair of wrought iron armchairs. The finely wrought stucco and top molding in "zelliges" are original.

Azzedine Alaïa

Above
An imposing steel console (1930) bears a
group that typifies eclectic taste: painting
and drawing by Chaissac, photographs
by Cecil Beaton, Ptolemaic period terra-
cotta head, César sculpture (1960s).

Right
In the salon, Azzedine Alaïa has placed
two Ibo ritual dance costumes from
Niger on a pair of steel dummies.

An old block in the heart of the Marais, transformed into a vast loft on three levels, contains the small world of the most offbeat of the Paris fashion designers. In this composite space, Azzedine Alaïa's professional life and private universe mix. A son of Tunisia who arrived in Paris in the 1960s, this creator has retained from his Mediterranean roots a sense of conviviality and the subtle art of mixing genres. Hence, in his showroom and shop amid the cutting tables are rare and familiar objects, discoveries, presents, or mascots – a mosaic that reflects the personality of one of Paris's finest creators of fashion.

An original cage elevator
serves the three storeys of
the semi-industrial block
where the fashion designer
has installed his business
premises, his home, and
his collections; American
armchairs in green
patinated bronze (designs
by Johnson); 18th century
gilded wood bed; Tunisian
lion puppet.

Following two pages
In the center of the long
suite that forms Azzedine
Alaïa's drawing room and
bedroom is an aluminum
staircase designed in 1950
for the Maison de la
Sidérurgie, leading to a
minute loggia, where the
designer puts up some of
his most celebrated top
models during collection
periods. Against the
natural brick columns are
two Dogon cabin posts, the
one in the foreground
displaying an exceptional
hermaphrodite.

Loulou de La Falaise

Queen of the Paris fashion world, the creator of remarkable jewelry, and a veritable muse to Yves Saint Laurent, Loulou de La Falaise is one of the foremost fashion designers among our contemporaries to have adopted the Bérard style of fairyland atmosphere for adults. In her own home, she has thus invested the Art Deco content of her 14th-arrondissement studio with a vast crystal chandelier, mercury mirrors, carnivorous plants, Indian fabrics, and an overall candle-lit magic, a sight which tempts anyone who views it to utter the famous words: "Open, Sesame!"

Above
Placed on a giant poppy in the garden, a butterfly brooch in lacquered seashell, designed by Loulou de La Falaise for Yves Saint Laurent.

Right
In Paris, the studio boasts an enormous chandelier, a wedding gift from Yves Saint Laurent and Pierre Bergé. The Louis XV scroll bed, converted into a sofa and placed in front of Regency pier glass, reflects the crystal console, itself surmounted by an old mirror.

Following two pages
On an Empire console in gilded wood stands a collection of rock crystals mounted on gilded bronze. Cecil Beaton's portrait is of Loulou's mother, Maxime de La Falaise, as a child.

Michel Klein

The Parisian stylist Michel Klein loves contrasts and everything that enables him to escape from the capital. Within his house 18th century France blends with such things as discoveries from souks, precious fabrics, and furniture unearthed from the Clignancourt Marché des Puces or the famous Isle-sur-la-Sorge summer markets. His whimsical residence betrays a variable geometry, often changing its decor – and never lacking in ideas. Here, modernity is at home with all the cultures of the world. As far as Michel is concerned, his houses are less unchanging assemblages than valuable sketches for his future collections.

Above
In the master's bedroom is a bed with a wrought iron superstructure designed by Michel Klein and made by François Privat. Here is a collection of *fixés sous-verre* showing views of Hong Kong and 17th century Indian characters.

Right
In the dining room, there is red paneling with gold highlighting, a candle illuminated chandelier, and 18th and 19th century engravings hung in close proximity to one another to create a theatrical ambiance: English chairs (1910), with fabric roundels from Braquenié. In the foreground is an original Louis XVI oak half-moon table.

The drawing room is painted a color which plays between blue turquoise and aqua green. In the foreground is a Louis XVI bed converted into a sofa and covered in mattress fabric (Marché Saint-Pierre). The sofa and Louis XVI armchairs are upholstered in a Thorp of London fabric by the firm of Marazzi. upholsterers at Saint-Rémy. On the far wall are oriental paintings by Guiela and Scali and a pair of mirrors from the 1940s. On the floor is a large Persian carpet.

Above
View from a room constructed in
traditional Japonese joinery, overlooking
water in which carp swim. The garden
is planted with maples, cherries, water
irises, and rhododendrons.

Right
The house is bathed in light and
verdure, sumptuously serene amid
giant bamboos. Japanese "Imari"
porcelain vases sit on a bench table
by Christian Liaigre.

Kenzo

This most Parisian of Japanese men is a man of miracles. He arrived in Paris in 1970 to take the worlds of fashion and the street by storm with his joyous and colorful creations. In 1990, he decided with similar enthusiasm to put Japan in the middle of the Bastille district. Buying an old factory, he then devoted great care and patience to the building of a vast house that skillfully marries East and West. At Kenzo's, there is a strong sense of elsewhere. But where exactly? Who can say? Like his fashion, the house of this master of good taste is inimitable. A feeling of luxury, calmness, and sensuousness prevails and seems to characterize the house best.

Previous two pages and left
An exceptional drawing room with swimming pool opening onto
a second internal garden. Along the run of pillars are rest beds
and a bench table, all designed by Christian Liaigre. Simple
white blinds deck the glazed bays equipped with black matte
lacquered door frames that can be slid open in good weather.
On the far wall, hung close together is a series of engravings
illustrating the Egyptian campaign. The large elephant comes
from Bangkok.

Above
Japanese style bathroom; traditionally plumbed shower with
wooden accessories imported from Tokyo.

Top

Garden side, the drawing room is equipped with an inbuilt fireplace: three sofas, leather and undyed fabric by Christian Liaigre. On the right is a small oriental picture. In the background, on a Liaigre console is a lamp in molded glass and a large 18th century celadon porcelain Chinese vase.

Above

In the small sycamore lined bathroom a marble washbasin has been fitted. Mirrors hide the closets. The small modular openings lighting the room can be conjured away by translucent canvas covers fixed on rods.

Right

Marble fireplace in the office library. On the mantleshelf are two Indian pictures depicting love scenes and a pair of 19th century Japanese candlesticks. Above is a portrait of an Native American by Tzapoff.

Karl Lagerfeld

" **H**e came this way and he'll be back!" The protean talent of the world of fashion since the 1970s, Karl Lagerfeld can create confusion like no one else. None of his illustrious contemporaries has had so many houses. Nevertheless, every decorative creation of Chanel's artistic director is itself prophetic. Be it the rediscovered or revisited, the rejuvenated 18th century, or the dusted down romantic, the futuristic, or the minimalist. Clearly, if Karl Lagerfeld had not become the prince of the world of fashion, he would have made a most remarkable interior designer.

Above
Desk in the Pavillon du Mée, photographed by Karl Lagerfeld in 1986. Below a study by Menzel are four cut-out silhouettes forming lamps among which is Karl's face, a creation of the sculptor Patrick Rétif during the 1980s.

Right
The spirit of the Age of Enlightenment: on the wall, a silhouette of Mozart by Patrick Rétif; in the center, a bronze chair designed by Mario Vila. The walls and seat are in a percaline fabric by Karl Lagerfeld. Carpet designed by Leleu in 1935.

Following two pages
Karl Lagerfeld long lived at "La Vigie", a villa dating from 1900 overlooking Monte Carlo. Here the bedroom has a neo-Gothic decor, and the Belle Epoque furniture came from Milan; 19th century paintings.

Above
At "La Vigie". in the corner of the neo-Gothic bedroom is a rare French armchair with side flaps: Louis Philippe period *meuble d'appui* or chest of drawers.

Right
Louis XVI-style medallion chairs covered in silk specially woven to an XVIII design (Tassinari): screen papered in a grisaille pattern. On the mantleshelf are candlesticks in bronze gilt.

Karl Lagerfeld's library at "La Vigie". Between an 18th century *combinaison* table in mahogany and a steel stepladder is a rare stamped Roëntgen desk; 18th century chairs by Delanois. On the floor is a mid-19th century Russian carpet.

DEL TEMPIO DI GIOVE XIII

PALLADIO

ŒVRES DE BRILLO TERRY

THEATRE DE GROUSSAY.

A. Serebriakoff 1960

Eight Parisian interior designers *at home*

For most interior designers or architects, their own private residence is perhaps the ultimate test of personal taste. Whether as a field of experimentation or as the encapsulation of a style, independent designers' interiors encompass a wide diversity. They reflect the different sensitivities within Parisian taste, as it has expressed itself in France and indeed abroad over the past two decades, notably through the articles that *Elle Décoration* has devoted to some of our top trendsetters. The diversity of style and the ability to capture styles from all over the world are what give Parisian decor its true richness. It is always realistic and is a source of inspiration for anyone wishing to decorate his or her own home.

A book frontispiece by the painter Sérébriakoff after architectural caprices imagined by Emilio Terry. The famous 1940s *ornemaniste* was particularly keen on ruins and neo-classicism.

You get what you want when you do it yourself. Each of our Parisian interior designers has expressed his or her finest aspirations in their own homes. The result is a range of sensitivity that exists only in the houses of these great interior design fashion specialists.

There is almost no more disheartening a position to be in than that of the interior designer in France. Unlike in newer countries, such as the USA – where furnishers from florists to window dressers and from interior arrangers to architects are often able to impose their will without dissent – in France, those who are engaged by a client to compose a framework for living are deliberately kept in the background. If the work is a success, the clients receive all the glory, not least the lady of the house who has "worked so hard" with her "friend" so-and-so. For the designer rarely has clients, still less a family. He or she has only "friends", even if such affection is merely at the draft stage, before the ensuing compromises. Hence, in Paris one often sees an enormous gap between the personal arrangement of the house of the interior decorating "friend" and the work he or she does for others. All too often the ideas of the great interior designers are rendered insipid by prudent clients.

His or her own cherished home is not simply every interior designer's experimental laboratory, it reflects the periodic variations in the designer's own evolving sensitivity.

The style of each designer nevertheless does contain a certain number

One of the rooms in the earliest galleries of collections of the *ornemaniste* and architect Georges Hoentschel, Cité du Retiro, *c.* 1900. Top photograph: sycamore bed designed by André Arbus for his daughter Madeleine, 1947; cover and ottoman in red wool (Galerie Eric Philippe).

of invariables that constitute his or her own personal signature. Such was true of all the best *ornemanistes*, draftsmen, designers, and decorative artists of the past, those very talented people whose work their successors today continue to draw on.

Interior designers fall into two main categories. There are those who conceive a house overall, from the topmost ridge to the least doorknob. Their range of vision is more architectural than ornamental, and they are fewer in number these days. Like

Philippe Starck or Andrée Putman, their talents tend to be reserved for public spaces or structures, such as offices, hotels, stores, and so on.

In contrast to these proponents of the radical, unquestionable "total look" are those masters whose work is essentially with private individuals, who rework preexisting spaces, providing furniture and accessories in consultation with those whose dwelling space it is. This is a humbler, though no less necessary, task, which leaves less room for creative initiative than for the spontaneity of the heart.

Surprise is sometimes expressed about the decors of the second half of the 20th century, how they are so rarely "contemporary". In fact, antiquity plays a large role in modern life. This is a paradox with possibly two factors behind it. The explosion of the service sector and the unmitigated rationality of the working environment are essentially expressive of the dynamism of the enterprise. Who really wants to live at home in an atmosphere that closely resembles his or her office?

Then there is the rejection of modernism from the 1940s onwards, an effect of that great world conflict, World War Two. Not altogether justifiably perhaps, rationalist forms have been identified with authoritarian, or even totalitarian, societies.

When peace returned, domestic interior design sought to exorcize the shadows of the recent past by plunging into the eclectic romanticism of someone like a Madeleine Castaing or the neo-classicism espoused by the last great houses of decoration: Jansen, Alavoine, Leleu, and others.

The prince of interior decorators and their best client, Carlos de Bestegui, summed up the situation the following way: "In the 1930s, my drawing room looked like a bathroom. Today, my bathrooms resemble my drawing rooms."

Left: Jean Royère's drawing room, Rue du Faubourg Saint-Honoré (1947–8). Right: The 1970s residence of interior designer Isabelle Hebey: marble-topped coffee table; 1900 standard lamp with wrought iron stand and melted glass shade; Saarinen plastic chairs (in the background).

Alain Demachy

ost of the Quai Voltaire, where he runs the sumptuous Galerie Camoin with infectious enthusiasm, Alain Demachy does nothing by halves: the vast staircase and gray stone vestibule, the salon suite on the best floor of an 18th century apartment block. Antiques specialist, collector, architect, interior designer, and, above all, trendsetter, he aims to bring together, in a place conceived as a veritable private mansion, "things" one hardly finds elsewhere. A great traveler in time and space, this man of elegance imposes his own style on the various eras of the past. His is the paradoxical style of an inquisitive man in a hurry, whose curiosity is accompanied by a constant search for quality, for "quality" is the word that best defines this designer's approach. Time goes by. He is not ignorant of the fact. But he knows that quality resists the test of time.

In the living room, under the high ceiling, is a loggia bookcase. Around the sofa is what amounts to a small personal museum, including a collection of African and Oceanian masks. On the walls are originals by Picasso, Raymond Hains, César, Mimo Rontella and Miro, painters whom the designer has known personally.

225

Above
Bold dialogue of eras and styles on two marble topped *meubles d'appui* designed by Alain Demachy. On the left. Roman period libation objects in patinated bronze. On the right. 11th century Khmer torso and a group of 18th century objects in porphyry: pair of ink and wash drawings by the sculptor Laurens (Galerie Berès).

Right
Another view of the white drawing room (see page 224). There is a white marble coffee table by Gae Aulenti. Between the two windows is a Khmer statue: plaster chandelier in imitation canework (1940s): leather-bordered hemp carpeting on a black-and-white tiled floor. The courtyard-garden can be seen through the windows of this fine Rive Gauche mansion.

Left

Alain Demachy's bedroom features assorted pictures and photographs. In front of the original Louis XVI wardrobe is a screen covered in a Polynesian fabric. On either side of the bed, Chinese porcelain vases have been converted into lamps; Art Deco carpet.

Above

Opposite the bed is this still life, in which every object contributes to the symmetry. On the table are two terra-cotta vases by Jean-Charles Moreux. Feather headdress made by Brazilian Indians.

Above

In Alain Demachy's dining room, a rare 16th century Venetian mirror comprising 30 convex "witch's pieces" in an eglomise frame is fixed above a Venetian glass ewer mounted on bronze (17th century), placed on an 18th century giltwood console in the Delafosse taste (former collection of Michel Meyer). Door architrave painted for optical illusory effect by Briganti.

Right

Green, bronze, and gold harmonize in this small dining room, which Alain Demachy has brightened up with a play of reflections between the 18th century Venetian mirrors and the crystal candleholders; pair of 18th century Chinese glass wall lights; in between, a man's pectoral, Nepalese (16th century).

Andrée Putman

From Paris to New York she is known as "the Great Lady of Style". Andrée Putman, with a youthful zest for life, embodies the faultless rigor of someone almost militant in defense of the modern arts, for everything — whenever it happened — of the future. She, for whom the history of design holds no secrets, mixes the cubism of Art Deco mobiles with the volutes of Thonet chairs; a particular plastic Bakelite lamp with a silver casket; a Cycladic idol with early gouaches by Bram Van Velde. Andrée, who is interested in everything, has had connections with the finest artists of our era, and continues to connect and support many of today's new talents. She exemplifies to all Paris the sort of rare patron whose morning gymnastics begins with an exercise of admiration for life.

Madame Putman's ebony desk was designed in the early 1920s for a collaborator of Jeanne Lanvin, the sketcher Drian, whose name is inlaid in ivory marquetry in the foreground; "Jumo" collapsible lamp.

Previous two pages

A Dupré-Lafon table defines the dining room area. It is surrounded by chairs designed by Dupré-Lafon, and made by Brandt. On the table are a trumpet in blown glass, an 18th century virtuoso piece, and two Louis XIV chandeliers. Right, are two Alechinsky canvases; end wall, over the sofa on the left, canvas by Bram van Velde.

Above

There is always light in this kitchen, which opens onto the terrace: during the day, light comes through the vast area of glass and at night from simple counter-weight farm lamps. Under a variety of pictures hung English-style, including works by Niki de Saint-Phalle and Bram van Velde, are chairs by Kohn and to the left of the entrance door, a Thonet armchair.

Right, top

In the corner of the drawing room, under a well of light, painters who have made an impression on Andrée Putman: Bram van Velde (left) and Alechinsky (right): black marble tortoise by Max Ernst and Ruhlmann armchair.

Right, bottom

Around a coffee table are armchairs designed for Sarah Bernhardt: glasses by A. Putman, for Krug. On top of the white tiled bookshelves are: Japanese lacquer flower holder, a Japanese box, mother-of-pearl candle holders, two Max Ernst sculptures.

Following two pages

Embroidered 19th century blinds ensure privacy for this bathroom. There is old faucet work and an office stamp on the tiled draining area; sculpture by Niki de Saint-Phalle; satellite mirror by Eileen Gray on the wall.

Jacques Grange

Friend and adviser to the great of this world, Jacques Grange's presence is a must for any successful evening in Paris. It is no coincidence that he lives in the very Palais Royal apartment, on the best floor, that Colette once rented. Familiar with the celebrities of his own time, Jacques Grange can easily relate to the world of Colette's *Claudine* stories, which he knows by heart. His sensitivity to the art of mixing and matching is clear in his vast three-roomed residence, which reveals his taste for the 1930s – he was one of the first to grasp its artistic value. Yet it is essentially a Proustian 19th century that pervades the home of this authentic collector. Here, every piece of furniture, each object, has a history. Our host, too.

Entrance hall of the Palais Royal appartment. Over the neo-classical stone console,
bearing alabaster vases, are two small wall mounted consoles by Serge Roche (1940).
Pair of terra-cotta Luca busts, early 19th century.

Previous two pages
Colette's old apartment contains some of the amazing collections, essentially of 19th and 20th century objects, assembled by Jacques Grange. In the foreground is a metal pedestal table and a Jean-Michel Frank table; pair of gondola armchairs by Paul Tribe (*c.* 1910). Between two windows is a palm tree *secretaire* by Eugene Printzt; upholstered *chaise longue* (mid-19th century).

Above, left to right
Portrait of Colette by André Osier (1950); 19th century Russian chair; canvas by Christian Bérard and collection of *sulfures* once belonging to Colette.

Right
Max Klinger bronze head (1980) on an Emilio Terry chair (1940).

Opposite
Polish-style bed, 18th century, with an oil on canvas by Brion Gypsin (1961); foreground, right, ink painted furniture, 19th century.

Following two pages
Restful corner in the drawing room with this comfortable sofa designed by Decourt. In the foreground, head of Colette by Fenosa on a bronze Empire pedestal table. Above the door, painting by Christian Bérard. Low lacquer table (1930), made by Dunan. At the back of the room, neo-Gothic mahogany "Troubadour" screen (19th century) placed in front of tapestry in *points de Cornélie* bearing the arms of Princess Bibesco; creation by Eugène Boiceau, *c.* 1920. On the right wall is a self-portrait by Christian Bérard (1928).

Pierre Passebon

Schooled at a very young age in the world of open air antique stalls, Pierre Passebon was a trader in the Marché des Puces at Clignancourt before becoming a disciple of Jacques Grange and today runs a gallery with finesse and dynamism. There he combines all the 18th century quality pieces with the more unusual productions of 20th century decorative art (Noll, Robsjohn-Gibbins, Bérard, Paul Mathieu, and so on). Pierre Passebon's style, a mixture of modern rusticity and decided luxury, is cheerfully and soberly illustrated in the Touraine residence where he spends his weekends. This first exercise in style – more than simply pleasing – has persuaded Passebon to link his dealing in varied and diverse objects with a small interior design agency. This still new complementary activity has turned him into one of the profession's favorites.

Main living room in Pierre Passebon's house, featuring a fireplace designed by him. A pair of mahogany columns (to a design by Marcial Berro) each support a ceramic by Gio Colucci. Between them, over the fireplace, a group of Syrian tiles (Damascas, 17th century). On the mantleshelf is a Ponpon bronze owl and a ceramic pot by Georges Jouve (c. 1950); wooden box (19th century) with embroidered seat. In the foreground is an American adjustable armchair (Mission Style, 1910).

Previous two pages
Pierre Passebon's bedroom has a 1950s and 1960s atmosphere: bed and banquette designed by Jean Royère. Against the far wall, two "Marilyn" silk screen prints by Andy Warhol. In front of the window is a Charles Eames chair and a Jean Prouvé lamp. To the right is a fortune-telling fairground slot machine.

Left, top
Library: walls covered in original cartoon strips from the 1950s and 1960s; metal shelving (1930s office furniture). In the far corner is a Vincent Corbière piece of furniture (1990s).

Left, bottom
The wicker armchair and two stools were designed by Charlotte Perriand in the 1950s. The tripod stool was designed by the architect Adolf Loos in 1910.

Above
Guest bedroom: bed and three pedestal tables (designed by Jean Royère, *c.* 1950); on the right, armchair with footstool, Charles Eames (1960s).

Jacques Garcia

Unlike most of his fellow designers, who lead their lives in the media gaze, Jacques Garcia is discreet by nature and could have remained in the shadow of a clientele simultaneously attracted by sumptuousness and discretion. Equipped with sound professionalism and a profound knowledge of styles, this creator of atmosphere allows himself, more than anyone else, to be guided by the "spirit of the place". Revealed to the general public in France by the considerable success of the Hôtel Coste, which radically transformed the French way of tackling such an undertaking, Garcia suddenly became the man of the moment. Even so, he still likes nothing better, when work permits, than to take refuge in the expressly archaic atmosphere of the châteaux he restores and awakens from their ancient reveries. This expert doer is also an expert dreamer.

Gallery of Château Champs de Bataille, owned by Jacques Garcia, who has entirely covered and copper studded these shelves. On the top are four wooden photophores and a neo-classical alabaster vase; lanterns placed outside the château at nightfall are kept here.

Left
For his bathroom Jacques Garcia has chosen dark red, which
he has used also for the curtains around the bathtub; lamp-style
metal chandelier; bamboo furniture, late 19th century. In the
foreground is a seat elegantly equipped with wood casing, the
cover itself covered with *petit point* tapestry.

Above
An atmosphere of antiquity is created with neo-classical items
of plaster. Reflected in the mirror is the chandelier designed by
Jacques Garcia, also in plaster; seating English mahogany,
19th century originals.

There is an oriental atmosphere in this mirrored bathroom, which Jacques Garcia envisioned as a boudoir. One of the pair of consoles incorporates a copper basin. The faucet is copied from a 19th century original. The toilet itself is incorporated within an imposing reassembly of woodwork mixing medieval and Arabian style influences.

Above
In the kitchen, every item, even the most functional, evokes
the atmosphere and lifestyle of the days of oil lamps. There are
Delft-style tiled walls. Above the dish warming cabinet are a
mortar, a former water fountain, and copper *batterie de cuisine*.

Right
The Champs de Bataille dining room reflects the "Troubadour"
taste in vogue in the middle of the 19th century. The large
neo-Gothic display cabinet exhibits the best pieces of a
porcelain service contemporary with the chivalric atmosphere.

Philippe Starck

With his woodcutter's physique, love of the outdoors, and great sensitivity, Philippe Starck's greatest love seems to be the wooden shed. Inspired by those on Long Island or Cap Ferret, he has built on the Seine, downstream of Paris, a small four-storey construction clad in ocean blue boards. It is here that this unconditional partisan of good living concentrates on the activities of his architecture and design agency. Yet professional aspects aside, this interior architect has turned his ground floor into a superb pied-à-terre. It allows him to travel upstream by boat to reach the center of Paris. In the spaces clearly ordered by Starck one discovers the subversive disorder of his style, comprising ingenuity and borrowings from many world cultures. Furthermore, the immensely flexible personality of this free electron of contemporary style makes his house particularly engaging.

Philippe Starck's taste for accumulation is seen in his entrance hall. Cheek by jowl are contemporary African masks collected from the Marché des Puces. In the corridor, light colored wooden boarding matches the floor. Each picture frame is surmounted by an illuminating chrome strip.

263

Previous two pages
Philippe Starck's bedroom occupies a
whole floor of his building by the Seine.
The square bed, specially designed for
the room, sits in an alcove of untreated
timber board which includes a dressing
room. In the foreground, right, is a
wrought iron stove with copper balls,
and chimney after a design by Benjamin
Franklin (Godin): a cosmopolitan
collection of stools. On the right is a
drawing by Gérard Garouste.

Above
On the ground floor a vast room, with
glazed bays and Venetian blinds on three
sides, serves as drawing room, kitchen
and dining room all in one. Above, in
the chimney corner, is a *chaise longue*
designed by Charles Eames in 1948
(reedition by Vitra). Neo-Egyptian
seating and wicker armchairs (1950s).

Right
Philippe Starck's table was designed for
the Trois Suisses catalogue. *Chaise
longue* and office furniture are by
Charles Eames. On the window shelf
going right round the room are plastic
multi-colored lamps (Miss Sis model by
Philippe Starck for Hicks): Godin stove.

Living room, on the drawing room side: a huge mahogany sofa designed by Philippe Starck with mattress and pillows covered in white linen. There is a solid mahogany floor. The window shelf here has a collection of Vallauris illuminating ceramics (1960s). In the far corner, behind the Fornasetti teapot, the elephant armchair was created by the sculptor Bernard Roncillac in the 1960s.

François Catroux

He was interior design's whizz kid. In his early days, François Catroux was as daring as anyone, and the time was the swinging sixties. Somewhat calmed by maturity and having acquired great sureness of taste, he can now allow himself to handle all periods with a deftness equal to the refined demands of his elite clientele. He can be found in his own residence in the heart of the Faubourg Saint-Germain district. Opening onto the silence of a lovely courtyard garden, this town house has references ranging from Africa to the creations of Mies van der Rohe. Furnishing elements that François Catroux has himself designed blend with some rarer works. It is a masculine balance, softened by the unfamiliar. Catroux's style is one of warm rigor. His house is all hospitality.

Warmth and sobriety in the kitchen diner created entirely by François Catroux in oak. including the huge wine rack high above the table designed by Alinéa at Avignon: the table is surrounded by folding garden chairs.

Right
The walls of the main bedroom are covered either in plain fabric (Casal) or an Athéna striped fabric (Étamine), used in such a way as to form a chessboard pattern. On the left is a plaster standard lamp by Laurence Montano; blinds (Modo); electric medical armchair, covered. In the foreground is a solid silver *timbale* designed by Marcial Berro.

Following two pages
For his drawing room, which opens onto a fine courtyard garden, François Catroux designed a console on which is placed a sculpture by Van Stuck (1935). A pair of large pastel and charcoal drawings by Lambert-Rucki and colonial statues sit on either side of the fireplace, which was specially designed for this room. On the right, near the window, is a mask from Upper Volta.

Looking into the garden from the drawing room: stone imitation marble floor partly covered with a ribbed cord fabric bearing African-inspired motifs (Étamine); *chaise longue* covered in Mies van der Rohe suede (Knoll International). On the right the round table with *loupe* top designed by François Catroux can be divided into five; pair of 1930s lamps and contemporary armchairs covered in black ribbed fabric (Étamine); Venetian blinds (Modo).

Alberto Pinto

He is the most international of the Parisian interior designers, working for very rich clients, businessmen and women, or high society people. Alberto defines his mission thus: "I try above all to serve people with considerable obligations. By introducing a little fantasy and good life into their pitiless universe." Nevertheless, Alberto loves disproportionate spaces. Having lived in the Champs-de-Mars, in the inordinately large mansion of Paul Morand and Princess Sutzo, he now camps on the best floor of an apartment block on the Left Bank of the Seine. A vast succession of drawing rooms of palatial proportions: this interior designer knows how to apprehend space and subdue it to his own whim. Yet although these sumptuous reception rooms are kept for celebrations and friends, he himself lives and works in his bedroom, a long room which amounts to a good-sized apartment. Such is the life of interior designers, princes of the ephemeral.

In the large gallery of Alberto Pinto's Paris apartment, the cornice and molded doors are painted in an optically deceptive grisaille pattern. A bronze statue of Minerva watches over a 19th century Anglo-Indian pedestal table where rock crystal spheres shine on bronze gilt stands: metal painted lantern designed after an old model, in the style of a Venetian painting from the 18th century.

Previous two pages
The vast bedroom that Alberto Pinto has designed as his actual living room. It was made from a number of bedrooms, the partition walls of which were knocked down. The studied disorder that reigns in the room contrasts with its size. On the end wall, a piece of neo-classical mahogany, late 18th century: Dutch furniture conceals television equipment.

Above
In the dining room, hung with emerald green silk velours, is an enormous sofa, the provenance of which is the entrance hall of an Italian palace: it has been reupholstered in the same fabric. Chinese figurines and cornets in China blue on made-to-measure stands: painting by Jules Alexis Muenier: *"Aux Beaux Jours"* (1889).

Right
In the entrance hall, old engravings cover the outline of an invisible door: Venetian busts (17th century). The neo-classical bronze profile of a deity sits on an Empire-style mahogany pedestal. Portuguese armchair (18th century), recovered in embossed polychrome leather and decorated with chinoiseries.

Index of names

Photographs by:

Reports by:

François Baudot: 8, 12-13, 14, 15, 18-19, 20-21, 34, 38-39, 40, 41, 42, 43, 46, 54-55, 56, 57, 106, 110-111, 152, 164, 165, 176-177, 178, 179, 190, 191, 192-193, 194-195, 196, 197, 198-199, 212, 213, 214-215, 216, 217, 218-219, 226 (left and right), 227, 230, 231, 262, 264-265, 266, 267, 268-269, 278, 280-281, 282, 283.

Marie-Claire Blanckaert: 16, 17, 22-23, 24, 25, 28-29, 30, 31, 32-33, 48, 49, 50-51, 53, 64, 65, 66, 67, 68-69, 74-75, 80-81, 82, 83, 84-85, 112, 113, 115, 116, 117, 118-119, 123, 124-125, 128, 132-133, 134, 135, 136-137, 138, 139, 140-141, 142, 143, 144-145, 148, 149, 150-151, 166, 167, 168-169, 170, 171, 200, 201, 202-203, 211, 270, 272-273, 274-275, 276-277.

Barbara Bourgois: 93.

Jeanne-Marie Darblay: 86, 98, 102-103, 104-105.

Alexandra d'Arnoux: 220.

Laurence Dougier: 160-161.

Marie-Claude Dumoulin: 78, 79 (left, right), 86, 90-91, 92, 94, 95, 96-97, 98, 100-101, 102-103, 104-105, 204, 205, 206-207, 208, 209, 210 (top, bottom).

Franck Ferrand: 254, 256, 257, 258-259, 260, 261.

Marie Kalt: 26, 27, 44-45, 47, 60, 76, 77, 114, 126, 127, 162-163, 164, 165.

Françoise Labro: 120-121, 122, 156-157, 158, 159.

Marie-Pierre Lannelongue: 58, 59.

Gérard Pussey: 232, 234-235, 236, 237 (top and bottom), 238-239.

Catherine Scotto: 172, 173.

Philippe Seulliet: 146-147.

François de la Tour d'Auvergne: 220.

Laure Verchère: 70, 71, 72, 73, 174, 175.

Art Director:
Pascale Comte
Editor:
Claire Cornubert
Picture research:
Géraldine Plaut et Geneviève Tartrat

Elle Décoration is a magazine published by:
Hachette Filipacchi Associés
Production Director:
Jérôme Dumoulin

Plate-making: Offset Publicité
(La Varenne-Saint-Hilaire, France)
Printed by: Clerc
(Saint-Amand-Montrond, France)